Psycho

{{BEYOND THOUGHT}}

Beyond Thought
the
Peace of Freedom
Living without Hurt & Depression
by
RICH LAMAR

{INTRODUCTION}

Please allow me to introduce myself... my name is Rich Lamar. A former student of the prestigious Berklee College of Music with an associate degree in applied art and science.

My occupation is public speaker, solo artist musician, and songwriter. My birthplace is Buffalo, New York and lived in New York City, Atlanta Georgia, and Boston Massachusetts. Presently I reside in Las Vegas Nevada.

I am a humanitarian. My main concern and actions in life is to commune with humanity verbally, artistically, factually, and actually in contributing to setting humanity free from the psychological blindfold of deception.

This book is actually the written result of my memoirs, observations, awareness, attention and passion I've given to our daily life. The reason I said our daily life is because it's a fact humanity is psychologically interrelated.

Anyone who observes life with an open mind without any form of prejudice have, can and will discover the same truth I have. The truth exposing the deceptive conditioning that has been brainwashing humanity for centuries.

Therefore no need to be sanctioned by any authority. No need of experience, research, teachers, et cetera. All those have place and they groom humanity here & there, but have no place in righteous transformation of man.

Every human being is the story of humanity. We all share the same biology. We all share the same earth and oxygen. I am you and you are me. We are the society of the world.

This book isn't written in a traditional format with index, chapters, references & footnotes. I wrote this book to be in a conversation with the reader. This book will clarify that I'm not a supporter of standard format.

It's not necessary to be sanctioned by any institution of authority to learn correctly. This book will deeply go into the fact it only takes the correct observation to actually see how humanity is being deceived psychologically.

This is not a book of authority or direction. It's a conversation in relation to observation. Pure observation clears the mind identifying that all humanity is related psychologically. Therefore, life is about relationships.

The relationship that sets us free from our mental slavery by unlocking the doors and removing the deceptive prison bars created by a psychological blindfold of deception. A tight blindfold that has been conditioning us to accept our daily conflictual condition as normal.

We live in an evil world that thought created. Thought is limited and can't see the whole. Once we can see beyond thought we solve problems that has been created by thought.

My deepest gratitude to you for taking the time to spend time to commune with me.

My intent for writing this book isn't to attack, convert, shame, depress, accuse, disrespect or discourage anyone in any way, but on the contrary to uphold, encourage, and help set people psychologically free from deception. Where there's freedom... there is peace.

I feel every human being is important and should write their own book to leave behind. For every human is the story of humankind.

Brace yourself, but the truth is... most of the education you've been taught has been a lie. Your thoughts have been heavily conditioned to accept and not to question false authority. False authority can only give false security.

{{You may or may not agree with this book. Nevertheless, you will surely discover that what alarms you to wake up is truth setting you free}}
~Rich Lamar {Beyond Thought}

~~

{THOUGHT}

?? What is Thought ??
Thought is our memory from our knowledge.
Thought controls behavior therefore thought
is a controller. How does thought lead us to
routine behavior of conditioned programmed
actions. Let's look at movement of thought.

It's obvious thought is one of many functions
of the brain, but it's just a small fragment of
what the brain is capable of. What initiates
that function to where memory is controlling
most of the brains actions and non actions ?

?? How Does Thought Control Us ??

• This is the cycle of the activity of thought

that I refer to as the habitual cycle of (9).
1} Experience
2} Knowledge
3} Memory
4} Thought
5} Action
6} Reaction
7} Adjustment
8} Idea
9} Choice

First experience takes place, and from that experience one gains knowledge. The brain creates a consciousness that stores all that knowledge in memory, and from memory all thought arises. Actions based on thought takes place and from that action a reaction.

Reaction leads to questions & confusion of how to adjust producing the need for ideas. Ideas from confusion make the choice that gives birth to another experience starting a new cycle. So therefore it's never complete.

The cycle of (9) is the path of thought that is an example of conflictual movement. It's the movement of how thought controls all of our action & non action to routine habitual cycle.

This cycle is the psychological conditioning controlling the mental behavior and actions of humanity. We've become maladjusted to relying on thought. Trapped in this pattern of thought & action humanity has produced an incomplete way of life in society. A perpetual routine always seeking therefore never full.

Thought has its proper place mentally and absolutely necessary in our daily lives every time we study, practice, imitate, conform or follow any script. Thought is very necessary to gain experience, knowledge & education.

Experience and knowledge is from the past. It must be updated and upgraded, therefore its never complete. Consequently knowledge has limitation. Therefore, thought is limited.

All thought and all knowledge is walking with the shadow of ignorance constantly creating conflicts of confusion, choice, and dualism.

Thought being incomplete doesn't think it's incomplete. This denial creates self centered motive to control all things. This movement to control is always inventing things to gain, maintain & sustain total control of the mind. Therefore... Thought is a controller.

The controller is always busy due to the fact knowledge is never complete. Consequently thought is always adjusting its adjustments. Measuring and comparing all things.

• What does all this mean ??

It basically means that by knowledge never being complete thought is limited. Therefore whatever or whenever thought is analyzing it's basically adjusting its own adjustments. Observing, comparing, and analyzing itself. Chasing its own tail (if you will). Therefore... Thought has Limited Value.

Formulas, methods, systems, scripts, etc.. are all paths created by thought measuring in order to gain, maintain & sustain control.

All method involve the movement of thought. It's the system of teaching and being taught. Where there's teaching there is conditioning. Where there's conditioning there is routine. All routine will create mechanical functions producing boredom and resistance.

Thought inevitably will produce conflict. Methods, systems, process, formulas, etc.

all take time and they're created by thought.
Therefore thought is time & time is thought.
So consequently the movement of thought is
the movement of conflictual time.

Time is duration. Duration is measurement.
It's the space between beginning and end.
This is a reality. Thought is the controller.
Therefore where there's thought there's the
effort to control the reality of space & time.

• Let's look deeper into thought & time...

Thought is always measuring. As man with
his thoughts observes earth & universe man
has stamped the natural flow of the universe
with a pace, and labeled it time.

The universe is sacred therefore timeless...
Holy existence of no beginning and no end.
Thought being the controller it is will always
attempt to measure the holy immeasurable.
Consequently creating confusion, deception,
and disorder.

Whatever man creates & imagines becomes
conflictual and limited reality. Thought, time,
and reality are related. Thought is limitation.
Time is the pace of all limitation. Therefore...

thought is the reality of all time.

Humanity depends on thought in effort to transform itself inwardly and outwardly. You can see this in institutions, educational, and political methods & systems. Unaware that thought creates the conflict we all struggle with psychologically inwardly and outwardly.

All memory comes from the past. Therefore, all thought is looking back. So consequently experience, knowledge, memory & thought are all limited, because thought will observe the past, present, and future with old eyes.

Thought will interfere with mental clarity if not in its proper place. Being so fragmented it creates psychological imagery, opposites, desires, conflicts and disorder... because it can't see the whole. Therefore thought only has place maintaining & sustaining the past.

Thought is limited, but it thinks it's unlimited. It's from knowledge that is never complete. Psychologically we're conditioned to rely on thought to solve all our problems but relying on thought is seeking order from disorder.

This disorder is movement of conflict itself.

It's the self centered movement of thought
that has created major divisions in the world.

So consequently thought creates, maintains
& sustains psychological hurt & depression.
Therefore we must go beyond thought for
solutions.

We will take a closer look at the movement
of thought and time later.

Exposing the complexities of thought and our relationship with pleasure and fear will be a constant reoccurring theme in this book of observing and living life beyond thought.

{CONDITIONING}

?? What is Psychological Conditioning ??
Conditioning is the programming of thought. Our psychological condition is produced by our day to day psychological conditioning. Thought controls behavior. Where there is thought there is the activity of conditioning.

People must be aware of the fact they are heavily conditioned. Conditioned by culture, family, environmental atmosphere, schools, experiences, traditions, religions, et cetera.

Conditioning is an experience, and from that experience, knowledge, memory & thought forms a pattern of behavior creating present psychological condition.

Psychologically all humanity is conditioned the same. {What !?! How can that be true !?!} I understand if that's your reaction to that statement, but let's look at that statement...

• Let's take a closer look at this...

This book is about taking that closer look by observing life and ourselves to see, unfold & discover the facts of our {Now}. To perceive {What is} taking place inwardly & outwardly.

Our common denominator of conditioning is pleasure & fear. The reward & punishment of pleasure & fear has been the conditioning of humanity for centuries in society to this day.

We must not confuse the yin & yang or the conditioning of pleasure & fear to be by any means necessary in life for order to exist.

{PLEASURE & FEAR}

Two major things all humanity is conditioned by is pleasure and fear. There are many fears and there are many pleasures. There are all different kinds of pleasures and fears just as there are many kinds of people.

Despite all the diversity pleasure is pleasure and fear is fear. It's not my pleasure or yours. It's not your fear or mine. The behavior of all people all over the world has been and being conditioned by the reward & punishment of pleasure & fear.

• Let's look closer at pleasure... What is it ??

Pleasure is movement of thought trying to control a sensation of immense satisfaction. Related to please... it's desire to be pleased. It's been called joy but it's not related to joy. Pleasure can be invited. Joy can't be invited.

Joy is a righteous response beyond thought related to the wholeness of righteousness. Pleasure is created by thought in relation to time, self, fear, want, image, and desire.

Thought again being the controller will take your feeling of sensation and create a crave for it again producing want, image & desire.

• Desire ?? Let's take a closer look at it... Desire comes from the following activity of Perception, Contact, Sensation & Thought...

• Let's observe how desire is born.

1} Perception: your walking down the street then you see a beautiful watch displayed in the window of a jewelry store.

2} Contact: you walk in the store approach the salesman and ask to try it on... you do.

3} Sensation: when the watch is on your wrist you get an immense sensation.

4} Thought: thought creates time in the form of inpatients by increasing the feeling to gain control of sensation giving birth to DESIRE.

Desire is the will of self interest. Thought the controller... is self centered movement.

Desire has plans of its own to fulfill what it wants by any means necessary. Created by the conflictual war of emptiness within the {Self}. The {Self} is never satisfied therefore never full.

• Let's look at {Self} with all its complexity... and disorder.

The {Self} is the {Me}. The movement of thought & time. {Self} is the self centered action and non action that destroys unity. {Self} is an abomination. {Self} is the enemy.

Self centered movement is the movement of self interest. {Self} interest is {Root of all Evil}.

The {Self} is Guilty.

The {Self} is division... therefore, the {Self} is conflict. Never full so consequently never satisfied. Where {Self} is... there is disorder.

It's constantly at war dividing unity seeking and fighting with its sword of desire. Riding the horse of limited thought & time. Always seeking creating struggle to achieve crowns of pleasure.

It never sleeps it's the pursuit of perfection and the conscience of vain dreams & image. Competitive and aggressively seeking to be pleased in constant aim to fill its bottomless pit full of desires.

The {Self} represents the conflict of time in inpatient behavior based on pleasure & fear. There is no time or conflict within patients. On the contrary inpatients is conflict of time.

The more you desire the more you will seek to be pleased. The more you seek pleasure the more you will fear pleasure will not be fulfilled.

Pleasure and fear is the movement of {Self}.

{Self} has the same identity as thought and time. Thought, time & self is one conflictual movement.

Therefore the {Self} divides. It fragments us preventing us from seeing the wholeness of righteous unity. Consequently creating the selfish {Me} of conflict, limitation, and death.

{Self} is conflictual & temporary due to being an abomination to the truth that sustains all harmonious righteous unity.

• Let's take a closer look at this...

Life is about relationships. To communicate harmoniously sharing all righteous freedom. To divide this unity creates conflict.

Where there's conflict... there is limitation. and where there's limitation there is thought and time. {Self} or {Me} is the manifestation of division, conflict, thought, and time.

Undivided love, truth, freedom, and peace is wholeness of righteous harmonious action. Therefore love, truth, freedom, and peace has no division, conflict, thought, time & self. Righteousness is whole. Self is fragmented.

Self is consumed with self... therefore self is only concerned with itself. The {Self} is fear. Life is about relationships. Relationships are the key to a peaceful society. Society is sick. The cause of the sickness is self interest.

It's impossible for any relationship to be in unity if self interest is involved. Therefore, where there's self... there is self interest.

Self interest is the root of all evil, because it gives birth to every evil work. It's the center of all image, desire, pleasure, thought, time, and fear.

~FEAR~

If fear was an ice cream parlor it would have all flavors. But seriously there's not a more serious problem to humanity psychologically than fear.

Everyone has experienced some sort of fear. Fear of flying, fear of snakes, fear of death, fear of aging, fear of losing a job, et cetera.

?? How Does Fear Arise ??

Fear arises from thought when what is sure becomes unsure. For example you become sure about your job then dualism of thought arise and time goes by as you begin to think what if I lose my job..? Creating an insecurity that gives birth to fear.

Thinking is time & time creates many fears. Thinking in the present of the past or future creates fear. You think of a terrible mistake from the past fearing it might happen again.

Therefore fear is an escape artist a master of disguise. Fear escapes the present {Now} in hope, faith, and belief. Thinking about your future will create fears. I hope I will graduate. I must have faith to succeed. I must believe.

Where there's hope, faith, and belief there's sorrow, suffering, image, hurt & depression. This is the deception of fear, because fear wants to control you. Fear origin is thought.

Fear can not exist alone. Fear must be fed.
Fear is always in relation to something else.
Where there's seeking and pleasure there is
the shadow pain & fear.

• Let's take a closer look at this...

If: Pleasure is interrupted...
Then: Hurt & pain is born.

• The thought of pleasure being interrupted is
the FEAR of hurt & pain happening again.

Fear feeds off conflict. All thought is conflict.
So consequently thought will increase fear.
Conditioned by fear in one way or another
nothing will make us think more than fear.
Thought is over active when we are afraid.

Remember thought is limited. Fear is a tool
of the limitation of thought. Where there's
limitation there's the movement of thought,
time, and self.

Where there's self there is insecurity. Where
there's insecurity... there is fear. Therefore...
where there's fear there is disorder.

Thought has (6) major tools of limitation.
Time, Self, Image, Desire, Pleasure & Fear.
Along with thought these tools make up the
Seven of Limitation.

These tools construct the mechanical man.
All forms of hurt and depression are results
of a mechanical psychological breakdown.

All living is energy, action, and vibration.
Righteous energy is pure, free and unlimited.
Mechanical energy is conflictual and limited.

Life is free and flexible. Mechanical action is
thought along with time, self, image, desire,
pleasure and fear.

Seven of limitation have the same address.
All occupy the same space. They all work
together to perpetuate disorder. They con,
manipulate, infect, blindfold, and deceive.
Whenever you discover one the others are
also present.

Those seven of limitation is our disorder.
Consequently this is what sustains disorder.

• Let's take a closer look... and simplify the

complexity of this...

If: These seven is the cause of disorder.
Then: The understanding of these seven...
is the ending of disorder.

{SOCIETY}

Society is a relationship between you and I.
We are humanity. This world is you and me.
Each human is the true story of humankind.
Just as the beauty of universal order shows
the order of the {Most High}. The disorder of
society reflects you and I.

• Let's take a good hard look at our society...

Society is basically an idea. A conception of deception built on a dysfunctional edifice of authority and routine where the people are heavily conditioned to obey, accept & follow.

In order for people to function at their best they must be healthy & free psychologically. Society conditions us to obey and conform. Conformity is an enemy to freedom. Where there's conformity... there's conditioning, authority, and routine... therefore limitation.

Limitation causes dysfunctional behavior. If your freedom is controlled your not free. Society conditions us to become something in life creating competition & fear of losing. This form of conditioning appeals to the self. The self is ego, competitive, and aggressive.

Therefore the self is always comparing itself to another. When one compares it's a lack of awareness. Where there's comparing there's fear, envy, competition, division & violence. It's all the activity of the limited self.

The self is division. Self is the center of the limitation of seven. It's conflictual movement

of the self centered behavior of self interest.
Society reflects our self centered behaviors.
So consequently we separate ourselves from
each other physically and psychologically.

The bourgeois, the aristocratic, the nations,
the religions, the sects, the secret societies,
the black & white, the short & tall, et cetera.
Groups & labels only help disunite the world.

Joining any group increases global violence.
Look what humanity has done and is doing.
We've become competitive & violent people.
This is why history is so bloody and violent.
Self interest {root of all evil} is the enemy.

We're conditioned to accept division & war.
We make learning about wrong things in life
a priority over learning about right things.

So consequently we know more about the
art of making war than art of peace making.
Our society is a military system. A lifestyle of
obeying authority and conforming to routine.

Conditioning, authority, and routine creates
mechanical behavior. The brain will atrophy
when behavior stays in a day to day routine.
This is disorder. Therefore... society is sick.

Conforming to authority makes one depend
heavily on authority. So dependent to where
maladjustment sets in to the extent you are
programmed to accept and not to question.

Inwardly you struggle to be free. Outwardly
you escape your present misery & sorrow by
comparing & competing with one another.
So consequently society has become a very
aggressive and competitive fight between
image (vs) image and ego (vs) ego.

Society functions in limitation day after day.
It's a psychotic cycle of seeking and conflict.
This cycle is an energy draining whirlpool of
{Experience>Knowledge>Memory>Thought
Action>Reaction>Adjustment>Idea>Choice} ·

This is our society the so called {Real World}
a psychotic cycle of choices that only lead to
actions & reactions leading to more choices.
This is the result of deliberate conditioning.

Your deceived and programmed to be naive.
Conditionings deception by propaganda is
the major method of brainwashing a society.
Constant repetition creates habit that dulls
the sensitivity of awareness.

Consequently producing a man made mind.
Your taught how to think. It's conditioning
you to become unaware, dull, insensitive,
and mechanical.

A mechanical mind is a rigid mind because
it's trained to conform and obey. Therefore
unaware of freedom & individuality. It's blind
to insight beyond thought, due to the fact
that all its actions are based on thought.

Society conditions us to believe we must
become something outside of ourselves in
order to be accepted and be secure in life.
Your conditioned to think your inadequate if
you don't fit into society.

Consequently when you conform you lose
the understanding of you. So you begin to
seek the favor of society. You accept, obey,
and imitate to fit in only limiting who you are.

Trying to live life according to something to
become something will make you feel that
being who you are is not enough. Therefore,
your conditioned to want to be accepted by
society.

Unfortunately humanity is programmed like a computer. Your conditioned to believe your not adequate unless you follow man made rules of society and be sanctioned by man made authority.

From the day that you was born you have been conditioned to become something in life. Therefore you must be tough, focused, and aggressive.

Society is nothing more than an idea that is deliberately conditioning you to follow and fit into a monetary system. Your conditioned by pleasure and fear therefore you seek reward and live in fear of punishment.

You wear a blindfold of deception. We are being deceived. Controlled by money & fear to become something that only supports an evil monetary system.

College loan debt has exceeded credit card debt. Graduating in financial debt is not wise. Education has its place, but it has no place in the sacred righteous inward transformation of man.

~BECOMING~

Be aware your conditioned and programmed how to think. Fear has made us slaves to a sick society. So we say..."I must obey or die. I'm not a success until I am institutionalized and accepted. I must become something."

Behavior is not a skill or a mechanical tool. Books, methods & tools are use to construct mechanical things. Human beings are alive free and flexible. We are not created to be programmed and mechanical.

Mechanical behavior is disorderly behavior. Disorder must be cured. There is no such thing as disorder getting better. You must be totally free from psychological attachments. Attachment to image, self, pleasure and fear must come to an end.

Disorder is like a weed that must be pulled from the root. As the weed will grow back if not pulled from the root... disorder incubates psychologically within us in many different forms of behavior if not cured.

Transformation within man must take place. Only righteousness can transform humanity. This means being touched inwardly by the light of enlightenment. This sacred light is freedom from all attachments of disorder. It's the light of truth eliminating all darkness.

Trying to get better at behavior will involve the cause that created conflict in behavior.

People often say "I'm trying... or how can I"? Initiating {Try} & {How} will only create more dependency on authority. This isn't learning. Once you ask {How} you stop learning and become dependent on a new authority.

Teachers, preachers, books, theories, ideas, formats, methods, formulas, systems, etc.

only lead to more teachers, books, theories, ideas & methods. The cycle of dependency.

They all maintain and sustain a maladjusted submissive behavior. Committed to obeying authoritative routines psychologically keep your behavior mechanical, predictable, and dependent.

Routine will create boredom and resistance that escorts you psychologically & physically back and forth within a dull habitual lifestyle. Constantly keeping you seeking knowledge that lead you to adjusting your adjustments.

Becoming involves being total dependent on the routine of thought. This means following authority that naturally negates your natural gifts and ability. Where there's routine there's repetition and resistance producing conflict that only maintains and sustains the past.

{Now} contains all past, present, and future. {Now} is the result of the past. Actions now will be the future. Truth is the righteousness of now that is always the same. Unchanging undivided love, truth, freedom, and peace. This is universal wholeness of {Most High}.

{Most High} is the righteous light that is the transformation of man. It's an inward light naturally magnifying the intelligent action, and gifts within you. Giving you awareness of who and what you truly are, and blessing the talents of what your born to do and love. Therefore no need for seeking & becoming.

~DISORDER~

Knowledge is the result of all our experience. Thought is the response of that knowledge. Experience always originates from the past. Therefore, knowledge and thought is limited.

Knowledge is never complete and always in the company of ignorance because it's from the past therefore it can never comprehend anything that's not based on the past.

We have been so heavily conditioned to rely on knowledge as a means of social progress we've become slaves to words & Knowledge. Consequently we've become maladjusted to a limited way of life full of routine and habit.

Therefore your not an individual due to the fact people of society accept, imitate, obey, and conform. Brainwashed to believe in the politics of government, daily struggles, and stressful jobs must be endured in order to achieve order and security.

Following any leader will only lead you to be misled. Be you not deceived my good people leaders & followers are the most dangerous people on the earth.

{Authority} originally comes from the word {Author}. There is only one {Author} of the universe and that author is not a man.

Therefore man made authority is deception. Man made authority is invented significants.

It's motive is to control all of your thoughts.
All man made authority is false & conflictual.
False authority only provides false security.

When your conditioned by pleasure and fear.
Your a trained self centered pleasure seeker.
If desires do not materialize it creates hurt.
Pursuit of pleasure creates a limitation of (7)
thought, time, self, image, desire, pleasure
and fear.

Society has become such a psychotic cycle
of (9) and limitation of (7) we can't tell the
poison from the cure. The doctor, patient,
wealthy, and poor person all have the same
illness in our dysfunctional sick society. We
share a common denominator of conditioned
psychological hurt.

Consequently our hurt incubates within us.
Therefore, many types of known & unknown
neurosis will psychologically exist.

Doctors, patients, wealthy, poverty stricken,
etc. etc. Everyday people of society all have
a common denominator of hurt. This hurt is
the result of pleasure and fear conditioning.

Thought is the controller of this hurt due to

conditioning creating self centered behavior.
{Self} is division destroying all relationships.
It's all the fruits of the activity of disorder.
!! Don't be a Slave to Society !!

{RELATIONSHIPS}

~UNDERSTANDING~
Understanding who you are is understanding
the fact that you are the seed of humankind.
We all need the same oxygen and earth. We
all would like to live a full life of unconditional
love, truth, freedom, and peace.

Contrary to popular belief living a life in love
without conflict is not impossible.

Life is about relationships. We must have a peaceful relationship inwardly first before we can have a peaceful relationship outwardly. Peace inwardly is the freedom that gives you insight in life relationships.

Relationships must have action and where there's action there is understanding. Action of someone exposes their understanding. Observing action one gains understanding.

We have a relationship with family members, pets, neighbors, students, teachers, religion, et cetera. The most important relationships you must have is with earth and {You}.

What do you see when you observe {You}. In life we must look at ourselves without the image of our desire for ourselves. Maturity is being totally honest with {You}. If we don't we will be living in a world of make believe.

We must understand who and what we are. It takes serious attention, awareness, and intelligence to acquire the sensitivity needed to discover and walk with the truth of {You}.

Understanding is the action of righteousness

which is walking with wisdom & intelligence.
Not the wisdom, understanding, intelligence,
and knowledge from educational experience.

Walking righteously is not living with all the
restraints of rules & regulations of authority.
It's walking with a clear mind without motive.
This is learning first hand not second hand
learning. It's the undivided freedom of life.

A relationship means to be related in action.
The word relate means to recount or repeat.
To recount or repeat means to acknowledge
past action. Therefore relationship is based
on the past, but is their a relationship that is
not based on the past ?

Righteous relationships isn't based on the
past. Righteous meaning whole. A righteous
relationship is right and complete not based
on knowledge. All knowledge is incomplete,
because it derives from the past. Righteous
relationships are harmonious. This means all
things flow together for good.

When a relationship is based on the past its
conflictual. It's based on limited knowledge.
Conflict prevents clarity. This allows fear to
control your relationship.

• Let's take a closer look at this...

As we learned earlier thought is a controller.
Thought is the response of our memory, and
memory comes from knowledge. Therefore
thought will try to control all relationships by
knowledge. Thought & knowledge is limited.
So consequently relationship based on these
will have limitation and disorder.

This means the activity of the relationship
will be conflictual. Full of self interest, lies,
envy, fear and violent behavior.
Relationships must have order not disorder.
Therefore they must be righteous.

Righteousness has its own order. Order has
its own discipline. Therefore you will be able
to observe and give correct attention to life,
yourself and others with clarity.

Observation without using past knowledge
will give us new eyes of clarity. Knowledge is
superficial action in relationships because it
will produce methods, formulas and rules.
Consequently the relationship will be based
on the superficiality of image, ego, and gain.

To observe without image exposes the truth. This is true awareness. This is true attention. This is learning. This is intelligence. This is being mature and serious. Therefore, it's the action of understanding.

~ATTENTION~

Attention is the nourishment of relationship. Where there's nourishment there's growth. Where there's growth there's attention and where there's attention there is nourishing culture of compassion and care.

Correct attention begins with observation. This is looking without prejudice. To look at the fact of {What is}... without seeking is the beauty of watching. This is what learning is.

There's a difference between attention and concentration. Concentration is focusing on a fixed point utilizing thought. Attention is observing the whole with all the senses.

Correct attention to yourself is when you see yourself as you truly are and not the image you have or want for yourself.

Correct attention to your mate is when your attention is without self. This means all your attention doesn't involve any image you have created of your mate from your thoughts.

An honest relationship can not exist base on an image. Attention to your mate without any images exposes the truth of {What is}.

When the {what is} is exposed the truth is exposed. It is the facts of the relationship. Therefore, when your attention is correct your awareness of your relationship will be correct.

Superficial attention only produce superficial results. Just giving attention fragmentally to your relationship you will lack understanding in other areas.

Attention opens all the doors and allows you to see the whole truth and the facts of the relationship. Attention is a virtuous action. Correct attention in a relationship produces correct awareness, action, affection & care.

~TRUTH~

What is Truth? Truth is where the self is not. Relationships must be related in truth and not in self interest.

What is Self? The {Self} is the root of all evil.
When a relationship has truth there's is love.
When a relationship has self its conflictual.

When there's truth there's love and freedom.
There's no disguise in the truth therefore all
communication is nourishing and honest.

Where there's beliefs and motives there's
prejudice. Where there's prejudice there's
conflict, and where there's conflict there's
confusion, envy, fear, disorder, and violence.

It's a fact we need each other. It's our earth,
but humanity has created division on earth
due to {the root of all evil} self interest.

Relationships must be harmonious with good
nourishing communication. Our relationships
must be energetic and nourishing. Where
there's no nourishment there is no growth.

Society is self centered so it's dysfunctional.
It's impossible to have a good relationship if
most of your time is related to your personal
goals, projects, jobs, pleasures, desires, etc.

When your relationship is related to a future
image you are seeking just for yourself. You

will be negligent in giving proper attention to your mate. Where there's no attention there can be no compassion and care.

Without compassion there can be no love. Your relationship will become toxic. A toxic relationship basically is a relationship full of self interest, hidden agendas, conflictual energy draining routine, and vain activity.

Society drains energy therefore lacking the right action needed to nourish and sustain a truthful relationship. Society is superficially motivated. Success is measured by gain and a good man or woman is measured by looks, money, image, education & financial status.

Truthful relationships are free and peaceful. Peace & love isn't in the brain. There is no image, duality, envy or any attachments in peace. There are no selfish thoughts, no measuring therefore no comparing and hurt.

Self destroys all relationships. Love, truth, freedom, and peace is one without any fear therefore no psychological attachments.

When {Self} is involved in any relationship there's always conflict. Self is self centered

thought. Self interest destroys relationships.
The enemy of all successful teamwork... is
self interest.

~LOVE~

Life is relationships. We all must be related.
Related in love... not reality. Authority, rules,
scripts, teachers, paths, systems, programs,
etc. etc. is a real relationship but, not in love.
Relationships related in love are genuine
and full of passion and intelligence without
rules.

Action of love is the truth. Love doesn't obey.
Love is the light of righteous action that has
its own order. Love is always fresh and new.
When you love the first step is the last step.
Love has no script... therefore no scriptures.

• To see love in a relationship you must be
aware of what love is. If your not aware of
what love is... Let's take a look mainly at
what love is not...

Love is not Sex.
Love is not Hurt.
Love is not Fear.
Love is not Image.
Love is not Desire.

Love is not Money.
Love is not Violent.
Love is not Pleasure.
Love is not Jealousy.
Love is not Knowledge.

• Let's look mainly at what love is...

Love is Most High.
Love is whole. Love is holy.
Love is righteous. Love is order.
Love is attention. Love is passion.
Love is truth. Love is free. Love is peace.
Love is giving. Love is sharing. Love is pure.
Love is wisdom. Love is patient. Love is now.
Love is Unconditional Action beyond thought.

Relationships based on conditions or rules
will always be conflictual creating many
psychological behavior issues. Love is never
conditional, because love is pure and
genuine. All things flow together for good.

Self interest is the cause of all conflicts in
relationships. Conflict invades & disturbs.
Love is security that has its own order.

Love has no self. To love is to die. Therefore
selfishness can't dominate the relationship.

Love is whole, complete not divided. Love is the light of truth, freedom, and peace. The action of love is always timeless and correct.

When your mate truly loves you. They don't know how to abuse you, the children, pets or themselves in anyway.

If your relationship isn't peaceful love isn't there. Love, truth, freedom, and peace all occupy the same space. The awareness of this is the insight that's beyond thought.

Thought can only comprehend what thought creates therefore, thought can not see love. Insight is the light beyond thought that can see the the whole. Seeing the whole means to understand the whole picture, to identify behavior in all relationships.

Where there is love... there's truth.
Where there is truth... there's freedom.
Where there is freedom... there's peace.
Where there is peace... there is Love.

• Let's take a closer look at reading behavior in our relationships...

~SIGNS~

!! Nothing ever happens without a Warning !!
There are always signs... but unfortunately
we don't always see them. We must identify.

~IDENTIFICATION~
Identification is defined as always the same.
Once you can identify the warning & safety
signs you can identify danger and security.

• Here's an observation of what must be
identified in relationships.

{A} IDENTIFY RELATIONSHIP

Relationships must relate in communication
and action. Harmoniously related where all
things are flowing together for good. No self.

{B} IDENTIFY PROBLEM

Where there's self interest... there is conflict.

{C} IDENTIFY TRUTH

Observing what is actually taking place is the
truth of your relationship. The actual is not
the image. The image you want for your
relationship is always a deceptive illusion.
The menu is not the meal.

{D} IDENTIFY SOLUTION

The solution is always in the problem. This basically means whatever is controlling your relationship needs to be stopped. Fear can control a relationship. Where there's fear... there is disorder.

Understanding disorder is the understanding of order. When you can negate the disorder the clarity of order remains. A clear mind... can see the danger signs !!

{DEATH & DYING}

>{Death is End of Action}<

The only thing we all can agree on for sure about our life is death. Death is the evidence that no human being is better than the other.

We all need the same earth and oxygen.
We all would see the same fact that truth is
beyond thought when our observation is
without any prejudice.
We all share the same fate of death.

Do not be deceived. Kings & Queens or any
other so called royalty or elite along with the
street beggar will suffer their day of death.

All humanity suffers the suffering of dying.
Death is not any theory or ideological belief.
Death is an actual fact.

Death has been sensationalized & magnified
various ways in books, horror movies, cults,
religion, et cetera. Untold millions of dollars
have been made filling minds with fear of the
phenomenon of death.

We are conditioned to fear and be sorrowful
of death. I'm not saying don't have feelings.
To be compassionate is righteous response.
Death is end of action. Life is action. Life has
instinctual action to love, protect & survive.

• Let's get a better understanding of death...

We can never get a complete understanding of death do to the fact it's very difficult to interview a dead person. Nevertheless, let's seriously look at this phenomenon called death.

The reality of life is death. This is a fact, but ?? What is reality & What actually dies ??

~TRUTH & REALITY~

Truth is whole with love, freedom and peace. This is the undivided enlightenment from the immeasurable and unnameable {Most High} to which there is no beginning and no end.

Truth & Reality is an actuality but not related. Reality is temporary actuality. Its origin is the thoughts of man. Truth is an actuality, but its only a reality in the limited thoughts of man.

Truth is Everlasting & Thought is Limitation. Whatever man creates or imagines becomes conflictual & limited reality. All thought, time, self, and reality are related.

Thought and time is the pace of all limitation. Therefore thought is the reality of all time as Truth and Reality are not related.

Truth has no path to it, but reality has a path.
All paths have a beginning, middle, and end.
Thought is cunning, limited & self centered.
Thought & Self is one conflictual movement.

Truth is whole. Thought can't see the whole.
Thought is a controller so it labels all things
creating a path to it and therefore limiting it.
Thought is always trying to control therefore
it has measured and labeled truth a reality.

Truth can see the whole. Thought can't see
the whole, but it thinks it can see the whole.
Truth comprehends reality. Reality can not
comprehend truth. All thought is conflictual.
Reality is thought & truth is beyond thought.

~DIVISION & CONFLICT~
Humankind is earth and earth is humankind.
Created to live harmoniously sharing earth.
This is the freedom of the nature of nature.
In universe there's no such thing as death.

Self & Death doesn't apply to the universe.
Earth is one sacred existence of life. All that is
living on earth evolves back into the earth.
Earth maintains & sustains its own existence.

Humanity is the enhanced crop of the earth.
Born free to abide in the fellowship of peace
with the universal nature of nature of earth.

Man and woman are blest with the passion
to multiply. Human kind is born free to love
harmoniously in righteous freedom of truth.

Conflict is the division that separates man
from the truth. It's origin is from self. In the
self there is no harmonious action. Only the
active self interest of self centered thought.
Self is abomination to truth.

Where there's thought there's limitation.
Where there's limitation there is conflict.
Conflict must die, because it's abomination
to the truth. Conflict only exist if there is
division. Where there is division there is
cause, conflict, thought, time, self & death.

All psychological attachments along with
everything physical in man inevitably comes
to an end in death. This is what dies due to
division and conflict.

Where there's division... there is conflict.
Where there's conflict... there's a conflictual
path of confusion, fear, hurt and depression

ending in death.

~THOUGHT & SELF~
The origin of self is the conflict of thought.
Self creates division & conflicts with nature.
Self is only concerned & consumed with self.
Self destroys all relationships. Self is the root
of all evil. Thought & Self is one movement.

Thought is a controller. A pleasure seeker.
Consequently misunderstanding of pleasure.
Movement of self, desire, image, and fear.
Thought is a self centered immortalizer. This
being so it's always creating time constantly
modifying itself to gain control.

Thought is such an immense controller in life
it immortalizes itself in death. Not accepting
the fact it is limited... thought immortalizes
the self by inventing numerous worlds of all
kinds of sorcery, reincarnation, superstition,
ghosts, demons, angels, heaven and a hell.

All traditions and organized religions are the
invented significants of thought. Humanity
has followed tradition & organized religions
seeking security and to fulfill pleasure. This
is primitive tribal behavior & worship of self.

All existence evolves together for goodness.
Earth is harmoniously alive and everlasting.
Earth sacredly maintains and sustains earth.
This is pure simplicity of Nature of Nature. In
the universe there's no Self or Death.

To hold on is the selfishness of self. I'm not
saying those who weep & mourn are selfish.
That's a righteous response, and instinctual
reaction. Dying physically & psychologically
is part of the reality of living in daily conflict.
{Self} is an abomination. {Self} must perish.

~HUMANITY & UNDERSTANDING~
Dying is apart of living. When we love our
selfishness dies… therefore to love is to die.

Every time we sacrifice something we die a
little. Every time we want or desire we die a
little. Every time we follow, depend, worship,
cry, pray we die a little. Every time we suffer,
struggle, compete, ill, stress, or under any
kind of pressure we die some more.

Our final resting place are called graveyards.
Their is nothing really grave about this yard.
We are from the earth… we return to earth.

Every person alive is the story of humanity.

The graveyard isn't bad luck, scary or evil.
All stories of the life of humankind is there.

Graveyards prove all humanity is temporary.
We all share the common denominator of the
reality we are limitation of division & conflict.
Death is the end of our conflictual paths of
pride, thoughts, and self centered behavior.

This reality is the psychological and physical
result of the movement of thought and self of
humanity. This is what actually dies. This is
the beauty of death. We must understand
this beauty of justice.

We must understand this before and after we
lose a love one. If it's misunderstood hurt and
depression can drain your energy to the point
where you will grieve yourself to death.

When we lose a love one it's heartbreaking to
say the least. We all must understand the
loss. As we observed earlier all hurt and
depression is a psychological mechanical
breakdown. Where there's hurt and
depression there is the involvement of
selfishness.

The sorrow of suffering over the loss of a

loved one is a natural righteous response. There's no hurt or depression in a righteous response due to the fact that righteous response is an innocent response.

In innocence there is no hurt or depression. In righteousness there's no self interest only action of understanding. When we lose a loved one we're losing the psychological & physical self of them.

The love they have for you and you for them never dies. Therefore... spiritually it's a gain not a loss. Whenever the self is involved self interest is trying to control our behavior.

> Thought Is The Deceptive Controller <
Where there's the movement of thought... there's the movement of self interest. Where there's the movement of self interest, there's the movement of confusion and want. Where there's the movement of confusion & want... there is hurt and depression.

All humanity is earth and evolves back into the earth. It's the nature of our mother earth. The {Self} of humanity must die. {Self} is the cause of our disorder therefore it's the cause of our division, conflict, time, struggle, fears, hurt and depression. Where there is a cause, there is a conflictual path leading to a death.

Love, truth, freedom & peace has no cause, therefore, it has no death. To misunderstand this truth is to misunderstand and fear living. If you fear living, you will fear death & dying.

~~

{OBSERVATION}

~LOOK~

To see is to observe as to observe is to see. Observation is looking, seeing & discovering. Look is to discover as discover is to looking.

Perception without deception from thought.
Observation is righteous action in the {Now}.

Observation reveals what is truly going on
inwardly & outwardly when using all senses.
Sight, hearing, smelling, taste, touching, all
energy of the brain, spirit, heart, and soul all
makes up the existence of the total mind.

Observation using the total mind is firsthand
learning. Learning from an experience is just
secondhand learning.

Pure observation LOOKS without prejudice.
In doing this what your observing will tell its
own story. Correct observation is LOOKING
without the self or any authoritative source.

Watching without the self or concentration
from thought will unfold what is truthfully
going on inwardly & outwardly. This is the
beauty of watching, because where there's
beauty... there's no self.

Correct observation exposes the difference
between Truth & Reality. Truth & reality is an
actuality but not related. Truth is everlasting.
Reality is temporary actuality. Its origin is the
thoughts of man. Truth is an actuality, but its

only a reality in the limited thoughts of man.

• Let's take a closer look here's an example

A mountain is not created by a thought it is created by truth. Thought has measured and labeled this truth by naming it with the word mountain. Therefore limiting every mountain. Words are never the person, place or thing.

When you observe with thought a mountain becomes the reality of the word created by thought. Blinding you from seeing the whole truth of its existence. The word has made the mountain a reality in thought not in truth.

Correct observation is humble action where there's no seeking or concentration. As we observe using new eyes that will open our mind to the clarity of awareness. Clarity of awareness gives birth to undivided attention that naturally negates thought.

• Let's look at what is unfolding here ??

This unfolds and exposes facts of existence Beyond Thought. This is being touched by an immeasurable unnamable wholeness that exist without the thought or hand of man.

When you are touched by the untouchable
its enlightenment. New eyes are open and a
sacred universal identification takes place.
Your no longer distorting facts. You identify
that the identity of truth is Beyond Thought.

Enlightenment of wholeness opens our eyes.
Exposing the fact that earth extricates from
all conflict and naturally sustains its own life
sitting on nothing in a galaxy of outer space.

Earth maintains and sustains its existence.
Therefore earth gives birth to all humanity to
contribute to maintaining & sustaining earth.
We are enhanced crop of the sacred earth.

In the universe there is no {Self} or Death.
Self and death is limitation. The universe is
unlimited. When self and death is applied to
the universe it's thought trying to measure
and understand the universe in its effort to
control it.

Humanity was created to abide together for
good. All life evolves back into the earth.
Earth and woman is mother of all humanity.
We are crop of the earth. Earth bares herbs,
fruits, vegetables, water, and oxygen freely

for our health and existence.

Humanity is enhanced crop born to be free.
We need our mother earth, but mother earth
doesn't need us. Therefore... be aware, we
mustn't abuse her.

Observe what our earth and nature naturally
shows & tells you and never ever question it.
Nature of nature is timeless righteous action.
Earth is sacred. He who understands nature
needs no authority, tradition or scriptures.

• Let's look at this... What is nature saying ??

As earth turns sitting upon nothing in outer
space by the righteous order of {Most High}
seasons change maintaining and sustaining
earth and all its abundance there of. Giving
birth to all humanity for all to harmoniously
share and enjoy life for free without division.

Earth, oxygen & water is for all life on earth.
There's enough abundance for all humanity.
When an apple is ripe on a tree its leaf is not
a price tag. Therefore no monetary system is
needed. Money doesn't make the earth turn
and no military keeps our earth secure.

Therefore money & military is false authority. Where there's false authority... there's false security.

Oxygen is the spiritual breath that fills the lungs of all humanity with life. Water is the colorless colorblind servant that purifies the health of all life on earth.

Observing the nature of the earth, sunrises, sunsets, and star filled nights in the heavens in its sacred glory naturally negates thought. Experience, knowledge, words, and intellect comes to an end... to a silence of the mind.

When the mind is silent it's without thought. This is actually learning firsthand. Firsthand learning only takes place in the present Now. Beyond thought is living life without a script or rehearsal. For all life is only actual {Now}.

When the mind is silent its clear from all fear. Great Silence from the light of righteousness takes over. It's the simplicity of sacred order. Order is the holy touch of the untouchable. It's righteous order having its own discipline.

When the mind no longer distorts & escapes {What is} actually taking place in the {Now} it is sanity. This is health. This is existence of wholeness beyond thought, space & time.

• Let's take a look at the meaning of all this...

Love
> Has no script... therefore no scripture <
Truth
> Has no path... therefore no pattern <
Freedom
> Has no time... therefore no thought <
Peace
> Has no division... therefore no disorder <

• This is the wholeness of righteous freedom that unites all humanity. The Great Silence of {Most High}. Absolute innocence of sacred undivided Love, Truth, Freedom, and Peace.

Despite all of our differences earth is home for us all. Earth is life and earth is very alive. Earth sustains earth. From the unseen atom to the mighty oceans and seas. From the microscopic mosquito to Mount Kilimanjaro.

The voice of the unnameable immeasurable communes with silence of the mind. When the mind is silent there's no interference at all from thought. Great silence of the present {Now} is righteous energy negating thought from distorting the facts of what is actual.

It allows the pure health of sanity to flower, because sanity is a mind that doesn't distort facts. Action of understanding takes place as meditative action sustains righteous order.

It's the action of pure wisdom which is the insight of intelligence & understanding. Not the intelligence and understanding one gets from experience, knowledge, and schools.

Insight is energy of virtue {Beyond Thought}. Virtue of undivided love, truth, freedom, and peace. It's immeasurable universal righteous action. Sacred innocent wholeness giving us the freedom of inward peace that naturally puts an end to hurt and depression.

Beyond Thought is not an organized religion. Its living with the light of true righteousness.

Therefore living firsthand... not secondhand according to the invented significants from the mind games of tradition, Kings, Queens, symbols or any other man made authority.

Pure observation opens the door to wisdom. Where there's wisdom... there is righteous insightful, intelligence, and understanding Beyond Thought.

• Wow... Let's take a deep breath... look at all this & break it down before swallowing.

A silent mind is a clear mind. A clear mind is without any interference from thought. This opens our eyes to see what nature naturally shows and tells us without the interference of thought which is the controller.

When the controller is no longer in control all fear comes to an end & you understand who and what you are. Interference and darkness will no longer distract your relationship with the universe.

A clear mind is touched by the untouchable where righteous universal order takes over. This is freedom from authority & deception. This is peace. This is the energy of love.

It's actual discovering without any seeking.
It's actual attention without concentration.
It's actual doing without struggle to become.
It's actual living firsthand not secondhand.
It's actual learning... by actually looking.

{MEDITATION}

~Silence of the Mind~
A clear mind is a healthy free peaceful mind.
This is silence of the mind. When the mind is
silent all fear comes to an end and righteous
order takes over. All righteous order has its
own discipline. This is firsthand learning.
This is meditation.

Meditation is not escape its righteous living
within love, truth, freedom & peace of Now.
Pure observation, awareness, and attention.

Looking at daily life actually not theoretically.
A mind that is clear and not from the state of
conditioned knowledge & thought. Therefore

it's not second hand learning.

Meditation is correct religion. Meditation is
the correct approach to order and disorder.
Living right is truth of religion. This means
walking righteously.

Meditation is living beyond thought. This
means living without being controlled or
dependent on any authority, books, fear,
gurus, traditions and organized religions.

Meditation is not fragmented or hypocritical
behavior of duality. Meditation is the sacred
energy of righteousness. Righteousness has
its own order. Order has its own discipline.

Therefore... righteousness does not escape
{What is} it's no struggle between {What is}
and what should be. No hurt or depression.

Meditation is not prayer. Prayer is thought.
Thought is limited and conflicts with truth.
Therefore prayer is the movement of {Self}.
Repetitively verbalizing yourself into a deep
emotional trancelike state creating hypnosis.

Regrets of the past and fears of the future
invents belief and prayer to escape all the

fear and suffering created by conforming to conditioning that breeds pleasure seeking.

We are conditioned from birth by pleasure and fear. Our behavior in society is based on reward and punishment. Therefore we seek pleasure. Consequently pleasure seeking is selfish desire that breeds regret and fear.

Meditation is correct attention. An action of humility to {Most High} without self interest.

In meditation all your senses are important. It's humble action therefore correct attention no seeking, no comparing & no attachments. It's the art of listening that naturally negates thought. Art of listening is pure meditation. It's attention without thought.

• What is attention without thought ??

Pure observation is utilizing all your senses. All seeking comes to an end as awareness of the present {Now} creates attention beyond concentration that negates thought.

Observing nature of nature in all its natural splendor of flowers, birds, trees, mountains and streams you gain awareness of sacred harmonious action in the present {Now}.

Within the nature of nature you will discover
the beauty of watching. {The Great Silence}.
This is an awareness of {What is} happening
{Now}. An understanding {Beyond Thought}
No fear... just the fact your one with nature.

The universe is harmonious with wholeness.
Love, Truth, Freedom, and Peace. No {Self}.
Thought is limited and can't see the whole.
Thought only maintains & sustains the past.

Meditation is life in the {NOW} not in {HOW}.
{Now} contains all past, present, and future.
This is being in touch with the untouchable.
Seeing the whole therefore vision to foresee.

Meditation has an energy {Beyond Thought}.
Living in newness of {Now} no attachments.
Therefore no need for seeking or becoming.

{HOW} is a form of seeking. Involving {HOW}
you involve methods, systems, and formulas.
Where there's methods... there is thought.
Where there's thought... there is limitation.
Where there's limitation... there is conflict.

Meditation is a humble action that naturally

puts all of your senses in there proper place. In order to do this all forms of seeking must come to an end. Therefore, all of self control must come to an end.

• Let's take a closer look at this...

{Now} contains all past, present, and future. {Now} is the result of the past. Actions now will be the future. Truth is the righteousness of now that is always the same. Unchanging undivided love, truth, freedom, and peace. This is universal wholeness of {Most High}.

Meditation is right action {Beyond Thought}. A clear mind is righteous and harmonious. It provides & protects without idea and effort. For all things are flowing together for good. This is not escaping {Now} it's living {Now}.

~{The Great Silence} of {NOW}~
is Past, Present & Future of the {Most High} undivided Love, Truth, Freedom and Peace.

Pure meditation is silence of the mind. When the mind is silent clarity takes the place of confusion. Therefore understanding takes place in the present {Now}.

A clear mind is not divided. Whenever the mind is clear without authority and method correct meditation is taking place. There is no system, no {How} or any instructions.

Involving {how} you involve thought & time. {How} is thought. Thought creates, paths, methods, systems, formulas, and patterns that create time. This is why any meditation involving methods is not correct meditation.

To sit and concentrate with hands & fingers adjusted, mentally focusing on a fixed point, symbols, groups, leaders, chanting, reading, controlled breathing, etc. all involve thought.

Any process of thought, time, instructions or an instructor is not correct meditation at all. Meditation is freedom from fear & authority.

Teachers and rules create thought, time, and authority. Where there's thought, time, and authority there is limitation. Where there is limitation... there is the disorder of conflict.

When walking righteously life is in order and all things flow together for good. Therefore the first step is the last step. No processing, methods, systems or formulas for becoming.

No need for authority, conformity or belief.

Meditation is freedom from fear. It is order.
Sacred energy... A mutation... A purification.
Walking righteously is true meditative action
of undivided love, truth, freedom, and peace
sustaining order.

Be still..

{RIGHTEOUSNESS}

~Living Right~
The word right means correct and from the
word Righteous. Righteousness is whole and
wholeness means holy. Holy is wholeness of
undivided Love, Truth, Freedom, and Peace.

{Most High} is existence of love. Absolute
immeasurable unnameable enlightenment.
The untraceable energy of all righteousness.

Therefore... righteousness has its own order. Order has its own discipline. This discipline is the righteous order that's harmonious with the virtue of love, truth, freedom, and peace. Therefore constant awareness and learning.

To be righteous is to understand the present {Now}. Action is understanding so the action of righteousness doesn't escape the {Now} it's living {Now}. Therefore righteous action is the solution to present disorder.

• Let's take a closer look at this...

Organized religions condition you to put your faith in the future. If you take a closer look at belief and faith you can see it takes you out of the present {Now}. It's not the action of understanding.

• Hope, faith, and belief is activity of desire. Therefore not the action of righteousness.

Walking righteously is living harmoniously. Therefore no seeking, comparing, hurt, fear, conformity, competitiveness or attachment. It's an everlasting light therefore eliminating all division and conflict of evil and darkness.

Anyone speaking, writing, or performing the truth is merely repeating truth that has been spoken, written or artistically performed in the past. Truth is an unchanging undivided everlasting light of past, present, and future.

All thought is movement of division, conflict, time and self. Thought is guilty of inventing all traditions and organized religions where one must conform to a script or method to be apart of. This is invented authority. One of the many blindfolds of deception.

Whenever one has to abide by rules, scripts or scriptures it creates a pattern or a path. Consequently paths are conflictual & limited. Conformity creates authority and resistance. Whenever there's resistance there's conflict.

Truth is where the self is not. Where there's self... there's thought and limited behavior. Truth has no path. Truth is immeasurable to which there is no beginning and no end. All paths have a beginning, middle, and an end.

• Let's look at what's being exposed here...

~To path truth is to trace the un traceable~
Truth can't be manipulated and maneuvered.

It's only one truth. It's not Christian, Buddha, Islamic, Jewish, Catholic, Jehovah Witness, Rastafarian or any organized religions truth. Truth can't be organized, retailed, and sold. It is insight, innocent, free, and flexible not programmed.

Walking righteously is the first and last step. Humble meditative action naturally keeping thought in its proper place. Walking without conflict. Living without any contradiction. It's innocent, and where there's innocence there is no hurt.

Pure observation, awareness, attention, and meditation is natural order of righteousness. It's the sacred rhythm of the entire universe. The energy of love, truth, freedom & peace.

Righteous action is meditation that sustains order. Living life first hand beyond thought. Righteous freedom is undivided therefore... not destructive.

It's not a second hand action created by the second hand people programmed to follow books & scriptures of invented significants.

No {Self} therefore no confused conscious.
No envy or insecurity therefore no jealousy.
No division and conflict therefore no duality,
hate, fragmented or hypocritical behavior.

Living life harmoniously without any seeking.
Pure observation, awareness, and attention.
Action that's not based on the past or future.
A relationship with the truth of life is the pure
righteous order of life which is the art of life.

{Most High} is wholeness of universal order.
Enlightenment of immeasurable existence.
Providing & protecting without idea & effort
from the thoughts & actions from humanity.
{Most High} is righteousness that is beyond
measurement therefore {Beyond Thought}.

{ACTION & SOLUTION}

~ACTION~

Action is the energy of doing. Therefore all of our actions are either positive or negative.

Positive meaning righteous unlimited action. Negative meaning conflictual limited activity.

All righteous action sustains order. All limited activity will only maintain & sustain disorder. Thought is limited. Action based on thought will only maintain and sustain the past.

Thought has created a society conditioned by pleasure and fear. So consequently our actions are based on reward & punishment. Therefore relationships become conditional within a psychotic cycle of action & reaction.

Conditioned by fear & pleasure will produce insecurity thus creating constant comparing and competitive behavior. This leads to man creating division of nations, groups & labels. So consequently an energy draining lifestyle that accepts and supports violence and war.

There's no freedom in a society conditioned to conform to authority. Whenever anyone conforms to anything they deny themselves from learning about who and what they are.

Consequently society is the activity of daily disorder creating daily hurt and depression. This is due to lack of the peace of freedom.

Invented significants is humanities ultimate escape from self created sorrow in daily life. Regret of the past & fear of the future has lead man to seek security in all forms of groups, traditions, and organized religions.

Authority, Authority, Authority... is the major tool used in conditioning you to conform and become a mechanical follower. Never follow. Whenever you follow you negate {You}.

Following any person, group, script, etc. etc. is living your life according to something. It's not firsthand learning its only imitating.

Society has become a major problem to the child & adult. It's an ugly fact that society is the result of people so propagandized and conditioned to accept and not question any authority. Consequently, your programmed like a computer. Your being controlled.

•Let's look at the action of understanding...

Observation in the present {Now} is correct action. Due to the fact that facts are what has happened and what is happening {Now}. Action mustn't be based on any authoritative rules or scriptures. Humanity must be free psychologically freshly learning firsthand.

Never live your life according to...
!! Anyone or Anything !!
Living according to someone or something destroys you. You can not see who you are conforming & following society. We must be free from all forms of deception to control us.

All forms of belief, hope or faith is escapism. It's action of misunderstanding the present {Now} therefore it's escape from the present {Now} producing activity that will always be conflictual and never complete.

Right action is always in the present {Now} and learning is always in the present {Now}. Intelligent action or non action is immediate. It's the positive energy of the light of love.

>Let's look closer… What does this mean ??

It means where there's light… there is no darkness at all. Positive flow of the energy of light eliminates darkness immediately. The darkness of deception and evil can not live in this light.

This light is the awareness Beyond Thought that ignites immediate action or non action.

>For example let's say your having a nice dinner with a friend then out of nowhere a cobra raises its head at the table. Action is immediate to avoid the danger.

This action should have the same energy of immediate action as if you seen the snake enter the door from across the room.

The meaning of all this is our action must be immediate when we see deception or danger of any kind.

Speed of light unmatched in the universe is from immeasurable unnamable {Most High}. {Most High} is the only author of the sacred enlightenment that can righteously transform all humanity inwardly.

This righteous transformation is the action of wisdom, intelligence, and understanding beyond thought. Therefore immediate action and non action that flows together for good.

This book is about seeing the deception in life, understanding and taking immediate intelligent action to separate from danger. This is the freedom from all blindfolds of deception.

This book allows all to participate in the pure observation that opens our eyes to see... unfold, and expose the science of deception.

This is the righteous meditative action that silences the mind to look, see, and discover with new eyes.

I'm basically presenting an opportunity for writer & reader to engage in psychological freedom of pure observation. This is done for us to discover facts and solutions together.

I wrote this book to be pure open minded communication between writer and reader. It's a book where we can purely observe life without prejudice or mind games… therefore, awareness and attention beyond thought.

Be totally sufficient walking in righteousness. Magnifying and sharing the light within you.

~MIND GAMES~

~Mind Games are Invented Significants~
All traditions, religions, authority, institutions, teachers, leaders, opinion, superstition, etc. are just psychological mind games. Planting seeds of propaganda & deception to control.

Thought is always adjusting its adjustments. Never ever forget thought is the controller. Due to regret of the past & fear of the future thought tries to escape its own limitations by inventing significants in deceptive effort to balance and immortalize itself in the {Self}.

• Let's take a closer look & investigate this...

All traditions, organized religions, and belief
is a blindfold of deception in order to control.
It's all invented significants by the controller.

Thought is limited. Thought creates dualism.
Invented significants grooms rough edges
here & there, but ultimately psychologically
will always create the disorder of hypocrisy,
division, conflict and violent behavior.

This is total escape from the present {Now}.
This is what traditions & organized religions
do. Man invents significants, authority, and
beliefs that gives him faith in the future thus
taking him out of the present {Now}.

Belief and worry are dangerous mind games.
Invented by thought (the controller) they
deceive and control our behavior. Therefore
thought will put pleasure and fear in the form
of belief & worry to escape the {Now}.

Belief and worry are the twins of deception.
Belief is an illusion of an award of pleasure
in the future as worry is an illusion of fear of
the future.

Life is actual in the present not theoretically

or ideologically in the past, present or future.
Truth of righteousness is beyond thought.
To be righteous is living life in total freedom.
Free from all of what thought has created.

Following authority puts an end to freedom.
Authority creates authorship that negates all
investigation therefore nullifying all freedom.
Walking righteously is living free and flexible.

When insightfully blind your blind to light.
Accepting, imitating, conforming & obeying.
Seeking in vain. Dependent on all traditions,
religions, education, labels, secret societies,
et cetera.

Mind games are the results of all the hidden
agendas of motive. An agenda to control is
the cause of this deliberate conditioning.
Paths created by thought seeking pleasure
and security. It's all false authority. Where
there's false authority there is false security.

• Let's look at some invented false security
  by thought....

1} GURUS
2} PREACHERS
3} MINISTERS

4} POPES
5} RELIGIONS
6} PRAYER
7} TRADITION
8} RABBIS
9} PRIEST
10} FREE MASONRY

11} STATISTICS
12} OPINIONS
13} PROFESSORS
14} BOOKS
15} INSTITUTIONS
16} TEACHERS
17} JOBS
18} EXPERTS
19} PSYCHIATRIST
20} EXPERIENCE

21} KINGS
22} QUEENS
23} POLITICIANS
24} DICTATORS
25} PRESIDENTS
26} NATIONHOOD
27} FLAGS
28} SYMBOLS
29} GROUPS
30} NATIONALITIES

......................................Et cetera...

• These are all primitive and tribal solutions
that only produce dependence on authority. It
divides & destroys clarity of who you are.
Invented significants leaves you dependent
on its aid. Being invented by thought it can
never see the whole. It can never solve your
problems permanently it's only a band aid.

• {Authority} originally comes from the word
{Author}. There is only one {Author} of the
universe and that author is not a man.

All man made authority is deception. So man
made authority is invented significants. It's
motive is to control you and your thoughts.
All man made authority is false & conflictual.
False authority only provides false security.

{SOLUTION}

REV☮LUTION

~Our solution is {Inward Revolution}~

As long as humanity accepts being heavily conditioned and governed by false authority humanity will continue to live in fear to revolt against that false authority.

We all can live in peace together without the need to be guided and governed. Whenever your guided and governed your under the control of deception.

We must be righteously united. This means all people living life with the clarity of truth.

Action of truth creates & sustains freedom. Truth is revolution due to the fact it liberates. You must be liberated from false authority. Our solution is liberation... not education.

All thought originates from knowledge and all knowledge is limited. Never ever forget thought is a sly controller. Therefore it will invent all sorts of invented significants to maintain & sustain control over our behavior.

The greatest diabolical inventions by thought to control our behavior is religion and money.

Religion and money has controlled humanity for centuries. They're the twins of deception.

They control behavior with pleasure and fear.
Where there's hidden agendas or secrets...
there is religion and money.

We are all conditioned by pleasure and fear.
Therefore our actions are always controlled
by reward and punishment. We must be free
from all invented significants !!

Peace inwardly naturally negates seeking
peace outwardly. Seeking peace outwardly
will negate inward peace. Outward peace is
when you make material gain your peace.
Outward peace is superficial false security.
Therefore, deception invented by thought.

We are conditioned to rely on education and
to seek outward peace without establishing
inward peace first. Education will only groom
here and there, but can never bring about a
complete solution to our daily problems.

Consequently society is sick. A perpetual
energy draining cycle of action and reaction
from the reward and punishment of seeking
the outward peace of material gain. This is
the activity of seeking order from disorder.
Therefore, daily hurt and depression exist.

Be not deceived we are humanity. We must live harmoniously together. It's the action of righteousness having its own order that has its own discipline. This is living with all things flowing together for good.

Love has no script... therefore no scriptures, saviors, sects, systems, symbolism or rules. Love does not obey any man made invented significants. Love is righteous order that has its own order and discipline.

Life is actual in the present not theoretically or ideologically in the past, present or future. You must stand alone in pure observation of life and learn firsthand and not secondhand in order to see {What is} actually happening inwardly and outwardly.

Anyone who observes the nature of nature without any prejudice can truly discover that a silent mind is a clear meditative mind.

This pure observation opens our eyes and allows you and I to see clearly. Seeing the fact that we are the world. You can stay as you are. No need to conform or compare {{YOU}} to anything or anybody.

This is inward revolution that eliminates the chains of fear that psychologically causes us to follow, conform and accept false authority without investigation.

When you conform or compare you become weak, separated and blind to the beauty of you. You are unique... yet universal. There's only one of you in the entire universe.

We are born free to live harmoniously with all humanity sharing our gifts & the abundance of earth.

When a man truly sees who & what he is by observation without interference of thought the enlightenment of truth takes place. The identification that truth is beyond thought.

Self centeredness of thought will no longer be in control of his action and non actions.

This is wholeness. The peace of freedom. It's the end of seeking... therefore the end of hurt & depression. It's the understanding of pleasure and where all fear comes to an end. Living life insightfully beyond thought.

This is order. When you have order you have

the light of righteous wholeness. This means light of righteousness beaming within you that gives you inward peace and meditative insight beyond thought.

A light that provides and protects you in an evil dark world full of self centered activity.

Nothing left to desire when your whole and no need to seek for anything because what use to be empty is now full. Therefore your no longer being controlled, no attachments, no becoming or overcoming. No conforming to man made authority or belief.

Your walking with wisdom, understanding, and intelligence of righteous order. Meaning all actions are genuine and flowing together for good.

Your actions is the wisdom sustaining clarity. Action of wisdom is pure righteous energy of understanding and intelligence. It's the pure insight beyond thought that can see signs of danger & expose the science of deception.

This means seeing the false in true, and the true in false actions and non actions.

This makes your observation correct in the present {Now}. A constant awareness and attention of leaning firsthand what's actually happening inwardly and outwardly.

You will understand the fact that facts are what has happened and what is happening {Now}. The future isn't a fact therefore the observation of {Now} is the understanding that what takes place in the present {Now} is the future. Therefore, correct action {Now} creates and sustains a good future.

All humanity was created to live righteously on earth. Living righteously is harmonious. No comparing and No competing. This is the constant fellowship in unity with each other. No conflict between what is/what should be.

Living righteously is good for all humanity. Creating {A WAY} or {PATH} to truth creates division. A conflictual way is always divided.

Some people express... "This particular way to truth works for me." They're unaware that truth has no path. It's not a guarantee it will work for them or another. Consequently this is the cause of all denominations in religions.

Righteousness is not about a particular way. It's harmonious sacredness of love without a script. It has its own order and discipline.

Therefore no reason for leaders or followers. Beyond thought is insight. Constantly aware and fellowship with light of righteousness. It's not living according to a script or path.

Life & learning is always in the present Now. No need to regret the past or fear the future. Hurt and Depression is the conflict of thought that drains your energy. The more you think the less you take action.

Thought is an inventor and controller. When there's no more controller all fear will end. Hurt and Depression is the fear of not being able to see your way out of a self created way or path.

Once one creates a {WAY} or {PATH} to truth it creates separation from what is righteous. Righteousness is the transformation of man.

~BOOK of {YOU}~

We must observe ourselves correctly to see ourselves correctly. Read the book of {You}. This means looking at {You} and accepting what we see as is.

• As is ??.... What does this mean ??

It means not categorizing ourselves. If you categorize what your reading about {You} you limit your understanding of what & who you are.

For example when we look at ourselves we

tend to say... this is good, that is bad, and that is ugly.

My point is we must understand that what we are is good, bad, and ugly. Seeing and understanding this creates the clarity that eliminates all confusion of denial & dualism. We must accept what & who we are as is... this is liberation.

Doing this is to discover what and who you are by looking at the total you therefore, you see the whole you and not fragments of you.

This pure observation shows you that {You} are the world, and order takes place as you naturally discover the disorder of {You}.

To observe without image exposes the truth. This is true awareness. This is true attention. This is intelligence. This is learning. It's the action of understanding wisdom. This is the inward revolution that clears the mind. This is being mature, serious, and liberated.

~~

• Let's take another look at twelve things we have already observed in our conversation.

{ENLIGHTENMENT}

1} Enlightenment is the light of {Most High}.
It's the harmonious light of all righteousness.
It's being touched by the untouchable. This
means living life in order where all actions
are harmoniously flowing together for good.

The grace of love from {Most High} blessing
the righteous of earth before and after birth.
Wholeness of righteous action therefore the
light of wisdom, understanding, intelligence,
and meditation.

Sacred righteous energy that ends conflict.
Insight {Beyond Thought} seeing the danger
of conflict. No method, system, process or
path to become or something to overcome.
No need of seeking, authority or experience.
It provides & protects without ideas & effort.

Insight is the light of love in truth & wisdom.
Vision from the wholeness of enlightenment.
Thought can't see this universal wholeness.
Therefore, insight is purely beyond thought.
Insight is deeper than you think. It's beyond
the superficiality of intellectual knowledge.

Insight is the energy of {NOW} never {HOW}
When you ask ?{HOW}? you cease learning.
Learning is to observe and discover without

motive or path of thought. Natural discipline.

{NOW} contains all past, present, and future.
Truth is whole {Now} yesterday, and future.
The wholeness of truth is the light of insight.
It's the intelligence beyond the intellectually
of knowledge therefore it's beyond thought.
Provides & Protects without Ideas & Effort.

{THOUGHT}

2} Thought is a controller. A pleasure seeker.
Consequently misunderstanding of pleasure.
An analyzer. Movement of confusion, image,
want, desire, conditioning, pleasure & fear.
Thought is the limited {Self} it can never see
the whole. Therefore always creating time
constantly modifying itself to gain control.

Be aware that thought is conflict & dualism.
Thought is your analyzer and your analyzed.
Psychologically and Spiritually it is useless.
Thought is interference for it distorts facts.
Creating psychological imagery, opposites,
battles, conflicts and disorder. Thought only
has place maintaining & sustaining the past.

{REALITY}

3} Man seeks security so invents authority in
nations, religions, education, politics, laws,

institutions, etc. are all invented significance.
Therefore, conformity & dependency exist.
Invented significance is false authority, and
false authority is false security.

This has become our reality. The Real World.
A daily energy draining whirlpool of pleasure,
pain & suffering due to the lack of freedom
created by conforming to invented authority.
If you accept authority or follow any leader
prepare to be misled.

Love, truth, freedom, and peace is one love.
Harmonious undivided enlightenment from
immeasurable and unnameable {Most High}
to which there is no beginning and no end.

Truth & Reality is an actuality but not related.
Reality is temporary actuality. Its origin is the
thoughts of man. Truth is an actuality but its
only a reality in the limited thoughts of man.

Thought is limitation. Whatever man creates
and imagines becomes conflictual & limited.
Therefore, Truth and Reality are not related.

Truth has no path to it and reality has a path.
All paths have a beginning, middle, and end.
Thought is cunning & limited creator of self.

Thought & Self is one conflictual movement.

Thought is a controller so it labels all things creating a path to it and therefore limiting it. Thought evan labels truth as a living reality.

A mountain is not created by a thought it is created by truth. Thought has labeled the mountain therefore limiting every mountain. The word is not the person, place or thing.

Truth can see the whole. Thought can't see the whole, but it thinks it can see the whole. Truth comprehends reality. Reality can not comprehend truth. All thought is conflictual. Reality is thought & truth is beyond thought.

{CONDITIONING}
4} People must be aware of the fact they are heavily conditioned. Conditioned to accept, obey, and never to question all what thought has created. Tradition, religion, authority and all conditioning was invented by thought.

This limited narrow tunneled path of thought is our experience, knowledge & conditioning. The further you venture into this dark tunnel you will be mislead to become maladjusted to following a sick society of routine action.

When insightfully blind your blind to light.
Accepting, imitating, conforming & obeying.
Seeking in vain. Dependent on all traditions,
religions, education, labels, et cetera.

{SOCIETY}
5} Psychotic cycle of actions and reactions.
Experience>Knowledge>Memory>Thought>
Action>Reaction>Adjustment>Idea>Choice...
>{Back to Experience back to the Cycle}<
~Seeking order from Disorder~

Deceptive leaders preach peace while they
prepare for war. Society is where we learn
the right things wrong & wrong things right.
Therefore we accept war over peace.

We are deliberately conditioned to support
war. Consequently the action of our society
is inpatient and violent. This isn't love, truth,
freedom, or peaceful behavior. This is tribal
and primitive behavior.

{DUALISM}
6} Dualism is the movement of thought that
divides. The constant confusion of choice
that keeps you adjusting your adjustments.

This division is major psychological conflict. Thought that sustains disorder in behavior. Its the insecurity and uncertainty of fear. A constant battle between image and reality.

Thought is a material process. Thought is time & measurement. All actions and words of comparing such as (getting better, trying more, most, and becoming) is measurement. This creates fear & dualism. All thought is a conflictual path of experience & knowledge.

{KNOWLEDGE}

7} Knowledge is many methods of imitating. Knowing is just knowledge from the past. All knowledge is from experiences stored in the brain as conscious memory of our thoughts. Therefore mechanical secondhand learning that is never complete. Consequently always walking with the dark shadows of ignorance. Anyone who claims to know... doesn't know.

{FACTS}

8} Facts are {What Was} & {What Is}. What has happened and what is happening. The future is not a fact. Therefore action {Now} must be peaceful for a peaceful future. Due to the fact that what's happening now is the future.

{NO PATH}
9} A path has a beginning, middle, and end.
Truth has no path. Truth is the immeasurable
to which there is no beginning and no end.

All thought is movement of conflict and time.
Thought created Tradition, Gods & Religions.
They all have scripts, paths, and routine.

~To path truth is to trace the un traceable~
Truth can't be manipulated and maneuvered.
It's only one truth. It's not Christian, Buddha,
Islamic, Jewish, Catholic, Jehovah Witness,
Rastafarian or any organized religions truth.
Truth can't be organized, retailed, and sold. It
is insight, free & flexible not programmed.

{FREEDOM}
10} A clear mind. No attachments. Clear your
mind from what thought has created. This is
the beginning of all freedom. Life must be
righteously free from authority.

{Most High} is Sacred Holy Righteousness.
All righteousness has its own natural order.
Order has its own discipline. Righteousness
is living in the present without any conflicts.
The understanding of pleasure and the self.

Walking without motive, fear & attachments.

Where there's righteousness... there is love.
Where there's love... there is truth.
Where there's truth... there is freedom.
Where there's freedom... there is peace.
Where there's peace... there is order.
Where there's order... there is discipline.
Where there's discipline… there is learning.

{ORDER}
11} Order is virtue. Virtue is beyond thought.
Beyond thought puts all thought in its proper
place. It's the understanding of pleasure and
the ending of fear. It's the natural meditation
that sustains order. Walking righteously and
living life in the present without any conflict.
Therefore order has its own pure discipline.

{DISORDER}
Misunderstanding pleasure walking by fear.
Living life according to authority. Unaware of
{Self} controlled by money, pleasure & fear.
Living in regret of the past and fear of future.
A slave to society. Living limited by thought.

{WHOLE}
12} HARMONIOUS / RIGHTEOUS / ORDER
A clear mind of understanding who you are.

Not controlled by money, pleasure, and fear.
No seeking, No comparing, No attachment.
Not living according to any kind of authority.
Having understanding of pleasure, free from
fear living with insight beyond thought.

• This list of some of the things we already
observed opens our eyes to what is actually
going on inwardly and outwardly.

{BEYOND THOUGHT}

~A Clear Mind~

~Beyond Thought is the first and last step~
Observation without interference of thought.
A pure righteous meditative insightful action.
Therefore constant awareness of {What is}.
Not living according to any kind of authority.
Firsthand learning from pure righteous order.
Not escaping the present {Now} living {Now}
~Beyond Thought~

It's not a second hand action and lifestyle of
the psychologically programmed that follow
books & scriptures of invented significants.

Beyond Thought is a clear righteous mind.
When the mind is clear it's free from all the
conditioning created by thought. Therefore
allowing pure righteous light of undivided
wisdom, understanding, and intelligence live
within you. It is the insightful order of love.
The righteous energy that transforms man.

A mutation of the mind that opens our eyes.
Discovering earth is you and you are earth.
Constant awareness of the nature of nature.
Wholeness where there's nothing to desire.
No dualism. Peace inwardly and outwardly.
Therefore no attachments and need to seek.

Living humble with pure righteous dignity.

Innocent without being controlled by fear.
Beyond thought is the peace of freedom, a
life without hurt and depression. Therefore
It's understanding the present {Now} and
harmonious with the universe.

Living with the secure fact that the universe
provides and protects without ideas or effort
from man. This is security beyond thought.

The society of the world is you and you are
the world. When one truly understands this
fact they truly understand the entire world.
No need for teachers, preachers, rabbis, or
any other conditioning form of authority.

Authority negates the freedom to investigate.
Therefore… it creates conformity and fear.
Authority is deliberate conditioning that is
perpetuating disorder. So consequently… it
blinds humanity from understanding the light
of righteousness.

Righteous energy naturally negates thought.
Wholeness of love, truth, freedom & peace.
therefore no need of seeking or experience.
Walking meditatively with the understanding
of pleasure and fear.

Thought is conflictual superficial knowledge.
Thought is limited and can't transform man.
Righteousness is the transformation of man.
It is immeasurable unnameable {Most High}
to which there is no beginning and no end.

The understanding & intelligence of wisdom
that's not from the intellectual knowledge of
humanity. It's from insight of righteousness.
Therefore a natural ability to see the danger
of conflict and the cause of all confusion. No
process or path of becoming or overcoming.

Righteous order will have its own discipline.
Insight that is sustained by pure meditation.
Awareness of {What Is} without escaping it.
No need for any belief systems or saviors.

{Beyond Thought} is natural meditation that
sustains the natural order of righteousness.
It's the peace of the present {Now}. There's
no regret of the past and fear of the future.

The grace of love from {Most High} blessing
the righteous of earth before and after birth.
The light of wisdom & energy of meditation.
Insightful light that's beyond thought & time.
Your own light shining inwardly & outwardly.

This is living life in freedom without conflict due to insightful understanding. It's action of righteousness. Therefore, harmonious action of wholeness.

Living holistically healthy. Having constant awareness. No desire to control. No seeking to perfect, because all things are flowing together for good. Therefore, no struggle between {What is} and what should be.

A life that is not hypocritical or fragmented. A humble life touched by the untouchable. Walking harmoniously with righteousness, and all actions flow together for good.

Therefore no escape from {Now}. This is the love, truth, freedom, and peace of life that has no path. It surely provides and protects without us seeking, praying or ideas & effort.

You can't find it in a church.
You can't find it in a synagogue.
You can't find it in a temple or mosque.
You can't find it in any college or university.
You can't control it. You can't fake it.
You can't think it. You can't teach it.
You can't seek it… !! {It Happens} !!

It happens when your no longer a slave to tradition, words, scripts and scriptures.

It happens when your no longer a deceived follower programmed and conditioned to serve the invented significants of man made authority. It happens when you understand pleasure & fear. What all this truly means my friends is... it happens when your liberated.

   !! {Beyond Thought} is {Liberation} !!
A clear mind that is not being controlled.
Undivided love, truth, and peace of freedom.
Living without any fear, hurt and depression.
It's the understanding of pleasure and fear.

Humanity will stay primitive & tribal if actions of understanding never go beyond thought.

Righteous Transformation of Humanity is…

Beyond thought. It's pure righteous insight

that exposes the danger & cause of conflict.

It's the wholeness of living life. No need for any seeking. No slavery to selfish desires. No psychological attachments… therefore, no hurt and depression. This means your walking insightfully beyond thought.

Insight is... Seeing the danger
Insight is... Seeing the danger of self
Insight is... Seeing the danger of fear
Insight is... Seeing the danger of thought
Insight is... Seeing the danger of pleasure
Insight is... Seeing the danger of authority
Insight is... Seeing the danger of conformity

{NOW}

{Now} contains all past, present, and future. {Now} is the result of the past. Actions now will be the future. Truth is the righteousness of now that is always the same. Unchanging

undivided love, truth, freedom, and peace.
This is universal wholeness of {Most High}.

• Let's take a closer look at this slowly...

The present {Now} is {What is} actually alive.
{Now} contains all past, present, and future.
{Now} is {What is} the result of past action.
Therefore, actions {Now} will be the future.

If: We change inwardly righteously {Now}.
Then: All conflict will come to an end {Now}
and order will sustain peace into the future...
                    beyond thought.

Light of righteousness is the freedom from
thought the controller. In this light there is no
darkness at all. A sacred universal light that
exposes all evil and darkness. It is whole...
therefore... holy undivided action of love,
truth, freedom & peace {Beyond Thought}.

• Let's sum up all of this and my purpose for
 writing this book... What does it all mean??

          What I'm sincerely saying is...

Life & Earth is a beautiful gift to humanity.
You are free to be {You}. No need to seek.
No need to conform or compare who you
are to anything or anybody, because that
creates the {Psychological Attachments} to
fear, want, hurt, and depression.

There is only one author of the universe so
no need of authorship invented by a man.
Mans authority is a blindfold of deception.

Wholeness of life can't be found following
leaders, traditions, organized religions or
being sanctioned by ivy league authority.
It's not a good job being a slave to society,
or gaining wholeness in life in the form of
so called success of wealth & knowledge.

Wholeness of life is the righteous light of
clarity {Beyond Thought}... that rids one
from conditionings blindfold of deception.
!! Don't Be A Slave to Society !!
~Beyond thought is the peace of freedom~
Peace to you all...

~~

~Rich Lamar {{Beyond Thought}}

37426218R00065

Made in the USA
San Bernardino, CA
17 August 2016